THE SWISS ARMY KNIFE OF RETIREMENT CASH FLOW

STORIES OF FREEDOM & ASSURANCE TO PUT YOUR MIND AT EASE

KEVIN GUTTMAN, M.A.

BMDPublishing@MarketDominationLLC.com
MarketDominationLLC.com

BMD Publishing CEO: Seth Greene
Editorial Management: Bruce Corris
Technical Editor: Brittany Smyth
Cover Art & Layout: Kristin Watt

Copyright © 2017 Kevin Guttman
BMD Publishing
All Rights Reserved

ISBN # 978-1547103850

PUBLISHING

Printed in the United States of America

The stories contained in this book are for illustration purposes only. The persons depicted herein are fictional and any resemblance to actual persons is a coincidence.

Every situation is unique. This book does not constitute financial or tax advice. Please consult a financial advisor or tax advisor regarding your specific situation. Reverse mortgage borrowers are required to obtain a counseling certificate by attending a one-hour counseling session with a HUD-approved agency. At least one borrower must be at least 62 years old. This is not an offer to enter into an agreement. Not all customers will qualify. Information, rates and programs are subject to change without notice. All products are subject to underwriting and property approval. Other restrictions and limitations may apply.

DEDICATION

This book is dedicated to the hard-working, freedom-loving, senior American homeowners who still have goals and dreams they want to live out and who want to leave a legacy for their families. May this book give you hope and show you how that's possible.

The net proceeds of this book will go to meet the practical needs of refugees, widows and orphans.

TABLE OF CONTENTS

ACKNOWLEDGMENTS

I want to thank every teacher, coach, and counselor I've ever had; you made a difference, and I'm grateful. There are some bosses I have enjoyed working with who have made me a better person. Phil Chinn is one of those who was more than a boss; he was a mentor, a friend, and a father figure.

Kris Jordan has been a tremendous writing coach and friend. Thanks for working with me to make this book a reality. You are a gifted communicator. I'm grateful that you came into my life at the right time.

My parents taught me to honor my elders, and for that I'm grateful. My wife, Sabrena, and my children—Rachel, Garrett, Anna, Natalie, and Abigail, along with my daughter-in-law, Janee—make life worth living. Thank you for all of your encouragement and support. And thank you, Rachel and Natalie, for assisting me with the photos for this book.

FOREWORD

This book that Kevin has written is far more valuable than what it appears on the surface. This is not just another financial product book, but it has the potential to change lives— maybe yours or someone you love who is over the age of 62.

A reverse mortgage has been maligned as an evil stepsister, when in reality, it is the Cinderella of the retirement world. Kevin and his team are changing the way retirement is done in this country. No longer the "loan of last resort," FHA reverse mortgages known as Home Equity Conversion Mortgages (HECMs), are fast becoming the "Swiss Army Knife" of retirement planning.

HECMs are not one size fits all. As you read through the book, you will be amazed at the many uses of a reverse mortgage that you never thought of. Of course, the major and most common use is to increase tax-free cash flow for retirees. But some retirees and their professional advisors are using HECMs to decrease taxes, increase portfolio longevity, decrease sequence of returns risk, solve long-term care worries, delay Social Security, leave a greater legacy in conjunction with life insurance and long-term care products, do sophisticated estate planning, as well as overall cash management of one of the largest assets owned by anyone in retirement. Some simply use it to enjoy life more by going on vacations and visiting children and grandchildren. Many fortunate wealthy folks are using the reverse mortgage proceeds to give away wealth during their lifetime, thus making a substantial difference in their families, churches, and charities.

It's time to take another look at reverse mortgages through Kevin's book—a personal and serious look at this unique mortgage for you or for your family. It may just make a positive difference, not only today but for generations to come!

Harlan Accola
National Reverse Mortgage Director, CRMP, CSA, RFC
FAIRWAY Independent Mortgage Corporation.

INTRODUCTION

From as early as I can remember, real estate has been a part of my life. My dad was a realtor and a real-estate investor. The talk around our dinner table each night was about the people he was helping buy a home. I found it to be fascinating. Growing up in Orange County, California, there was always something to do. One of my favorite things I remember as a young boy was going to look at property with my dad, as he purchased rental properties year after year.

Real estate was very good to me and my family. Owning real estate allowed my dad to retire at age 49 and live on the cash flow from his rental properties. Real estate also put me through college and graduate school without any student loans. When my wife, Sabrena, and I got married, we started buying real estate for investment purposes as well. I've been a big fan of real estate my whole life.

After graduate school, I worked for a nonprofit for 12 years. My role was to raise funds from donors so people in poor areas of the world could have clean water, medical clinics, schools, small-business loans, and so forth. It was very rewarding work but also a lot of travel time away from my young family. My wife and I have five children, and being gone 50 percent of the time was challenging. After much thought, discussion, and prayer, I left the nonprofit world and started investing in real estate on a full-time basis.

Eventually, I made my way into the mortgage industry.

The thrill of helping people figure out one of the most important financial decisions they will ever make was fun. As I listened to their goals and objectives, I offered them options to help them accomplish their goals and dreams, which I found very fulfilling.

Over the years of working by referral, I have enjoyed success helping hundreds of clients realize the dream of home ownership. It's been rewarding to educate them about home financing options, answering their questions, and making sure they feel comfortable with the loan they're obtaining.

So, how did all that lead me to this book? Senior homeowners in America are approaching a crisis. Today's seniors are the first generation who have to fund their own retirement. Many are house rich but cash poor; that is, they're concerned about running out of money in retirement.

This book is divided into the following sections: Housing, Cash Flow, Medical, Dream, and Legacy, to help you more easily find stories that you can identify with. We share stories of how American senior homeowners are using their home equity to live out their goals and dreams and leave a legacy for their family. Senior homeowners are realizing that in retirement they don't want a mortgage payment, and cash flow trumps equity.

Our mission is to offer seniors financial certainty, flexibility, and increased cash flow, enabling them time and peace of mind to enjoy their golden years. I hope you enjoy this book, **and may it bring you hope as you consider the possibilities a reverse mortgage can open for you.**

If you have any questions please reach out to me through the following contact information:

Kevin A. Guttman
NMLS #384936
Colorado Springs, CO
(877) 251-9709
www.ReverseMortgageRevolution.com
Info@ReverseMortgageAdvisorsUSA.com

KEY FACTS ABOUT REVERSE MORTGAGES

-You can eliminate your monthly mortgage payment, but you still must pay property taxes and homeowners insurance and maintain the home

-You can increase cash flow tax-free from your home equity

-At least one borrower must be 62 years or older

-The borrower always maintains title (ownership) to the home

-The borrower must live in the home as a primary residence at least 6 months a year

-There is no credit score requirement

-There is minimal income documentation needed

-Your home can be a single-family home, townhome, condominium (if FHA approved) or a multi-family home with 2-4 units, as long as the borrower resides in one of the units

-The home owes the money, not the borrower or heirs (non-recourse loan)

-The loan needs to be paid back when the last borrower moves out or the property is sold

-The estate or heirs have 6 months to sell the property with two, 3-month extensions if needed

-The heirs can sell the home and keep the proceeds, refinance, and move in or rent out the home

-If, in the unlikely event the home owes more than it's worth, the heirs relinquish the keys and walk away, unless they wish to purchase the home, in which case they can buy it for 95% of the appraised value

-Mortgage insurance makes up any shortfall if there's more owed than the home is worth.

THE SWISS ARMY KNIFE OF RETIREMENT CASH FLOW

HOUSING

THE POMPONIOS INCREASED THEIR PURCHASING POWER

George and Danette Pomponio couldn't stop bragging about their 6 kids and 14 grandkids, ranging in age from 18 months to 18 years. Two of their children lived close by, but the other four were out of state. The Pomponios had decided they wanted to move somewhere warmer and downsize from their four-bedroom house that required a lot of yard work. They'd always been ones who wanted to have a Snowbird lifestyle, and after a recent trip to Tennessee, they decided they wanted Franklin to be their permanent retirement place. George had grown up there, so there was family close by, plus they loved the climate. With the money from the sale of their home, they would be able to purchase a home outright and even put some money into the bank.

George, a retired mechanic, looked forward to not having the responsibilities of yard and house maintenance. Danette, a former school administrator, was hoping to find something part-time just to give her something to do. Recently, their long-time friends, Peter and Judy, had told them about a positive experience they had with a reverse mortgage loan and encouraged them to consider it. The Pomponios had reservations because they didn't feel that they had any money problems and thought reverse mortgages were simply for people who were down on their luck. Peter explained that he originally thought that as well, but their CPA had suggested because of the increased cash flow it could provide for them, which is usually tax-free.

George and Danette decided to speak to a reverse mortgage planner to see if a reverse mortgage loan was right for them. The planner explained that they could buy their new home using a reverse mortgage loan, which would give them an opportunity to not have a monthly mortgage payment, although they would still have to pay taxes, insurance, and maintain the home. Additionally, they would only have to pay a down payment of around 40 percent.

They might be able to keep some of their cash from the sale of their home to invest or perhaps even increase their buying power. Meaning, they could put the full amount they received from the sale of their home into the purchase of the new home, and the reverse mortgage loan would cover 60 percent of the purchase price.

Together with their financial advisor, who was a retirement income certified professional (RICP), the Pomponios worked out a strategy that could extend their retirement funds. As a result, they had peace knowing they were better prepared to not outlive their funds. It made sense to them, as they knew their children wouldn't want their house in Tennessee. Having access to their equity now was right for them.

The Pomponios are enjoying retirement in their new home. They chose a retirement community with an active lifestyle that has allowed them to make friends and have main-floor living that will accommodate them for many years to come. Their children and grandchildren enjoy visiting in Tennessee and creating lifelong memories. And, George doesn't miss doing yard work or house maintenance.

THE SALAZARS ELIMINATED THEIR MONTHLY MORTGAGE PAYMENT

 Robert and Debra Salazar met in the summer before their senior year of high school when they were working at the same restaurant together—he as a busboy, and she as a hostess. They haven't been apart since. To listen to their story, they sound like the perfect family: high school sweethearts who fell in love, got married, had kids, and bought a home. They had their ups and downs, but overall life has been good to them.

Their four children now have families of their own, and Robert and Debra frequently rattle off the many activities their children and grandchildren are involved in, along with proudly showing off photos. They only had one concern as they settled into retirement, and that was their $202,000 mortgage balance.

Their youngest daughter, Alicia, had decided to become a business owner and open a dance studio fifteen years ago. She needed help with financing the studio, as she didn't have sufficient collateral for the bank. Robert and Debra wanted to help her, so they decided to refinance their mortgage to free up some money to lend to Alicia. Unfortunately, Alicia's business never took off. It failed after two years, but not until wiping out all of her savings. The Salazars knew they would likely not be repaid and forgave their daughter of the debt.

While they had made extra payments whenever possible, being retired on a fixed income, at ages 66 and 65, respectively, the Salazars knew it would be another 14 years before their mortgage was paid off. Their $1,500 per month mortgage payment was something they could handle now, but it was tapping their funds quickly, and they weren't sure if it was the best use of their money.

They spoke to some close friends, Benny and Bea Garcia, because they had sold their home to get out from under a mortgage. The Garcias lamented the fact that they couldn't control their housing costs because their rent was going up every year. They mentioned that they were looking to buy a home and were going to use a reverse mortgage loan so they could be free of monthly mortgage payments, although they still would have to pay taxes, insurance, and maintain the home.

Sounding too good to be true, the Salazars asked for the contact information for their reverse mortgage planner to look into what help they could receive. They weren't sure if they had to own their home free and clear, but they knew that talking with a professional would be the first step. If nothing else, they thought they could refinance and maybe lower their monthly payments.

The Salazars met with the reverse mortgage planner, who explained the process and how reverse mortgages worked. Based on the home's value, their current mortgage balance, the interest rate, and their ages, they were able to qualify for a reverse mortgage that allowed them to stop making mortgage payments.

In many ways, the Salazars felt like they recouped lost time and money through the reverse mortgage. Those years of paying on the loan were now allowing them to leverage the equity in their home, while making it possible for them to continue living in it. They admitted that eliminating their mortgage payment (other than taxes, insurance, and maintenance) has alleviated some financial stress, allowing them to sleep better at night.

THE MILLERS MADE HOME MODIFICATIONS

Bill and Doris Miller loved their home. They didn't like the idea of selling it and moving into something smaller because they loved their neighbors, the neighborhood, and their church. However, the home wasn't working for them anymore. Bill, a former construction worker, was having a hard time taking the stairs to the upstairs bedroom. He had become permanently disabled when he lost part of his left leg in a motorcycle accident.

Doris was a bookkeeper for a home service provider in town that provided residential plumbing, heating, and electrical work. She'd been there for seven years, loved her job, and didn't have retirement on her mind. And, while Bill was 65 and happy to be at home, Doris was 56 and loved being out of the house, except when she was entertaining. Frequently, Doris would come home from work, prepare dinner, and then head upstairs to the bedroom alone while Bill slept in the recliner, as it was too painful for him to climb the stairs and too dangerous for him to go down them.

To stay in their house, Bill and Doris recognized they would need to make some modifications to it. However, they weren't sure how they were going to afford this goal and were concerned about using their precious retirement funds to reach it.

They went back and forth on whether to sell the house and purchase something else, but their overriding desire to stay in their home led them to consider a reverse mortgage. Unlike a home equity line of credit, which would require them to make installment payments, the reverse mortgage loan allowed them to tap the equity of their home without monthly mortgage payments during the life of the loan (except taxes, insurance, and maintenance.) It also offered loan proceeds, which are usually tax-free*.

The thought of having mortgage payments seemed like a stressful option given their single income and regular medical bills. They also wanted to wait as long as possible to start receiving their Social Security benefits. With a lump sum payout from the reverse mortgage loan, they were able to make the modifications needed to add a master bedroom to the main floor. In addition, they added a laundry room, so Doris didn't have to go to the basement to do laundry. This created significant main-floor living, which was the solution they needed, without having to sell the house.

Doris felt more comfortable knowing that her husband would be safer not having to take the stairs, and she enjoyed being able to sleep beside him again. Bill says that he didn't know he had missed his bed as much as he had, and found it much more comfortable than the recliner.

THE WATERS DOWNSIZED THEIR HOME AND CREATED CASH FLOW

 Luther Waters worked as a maintenance supervisor for a manufacturing company for 22 years before retiring at the age of 65. It was an industry he fell into after being laid off in his previous career as an equipment mechanic—his job for nearly a decade. He always considered himself someone who liked to fix and "tinker" with things. He loved home projects and had spent lots of time keeping his home in great condition. During his retirement, Luther was ready to have fewer projects, as he found home maintenance not as easy as it once was. However, he still wanted a garage so he could continue to "tinker" with the neighbor's lawn mower and, of course, his motorcycle.

Luther's wife, Danita, enjoyed working part-time at a florist shop. She always had a green thumb and looked forward to interactions with customers. She appreciated Luther's hard work and his handy abilities but was also ready to sell their family home and downsize into something that didn't require as much maintenance. She still wanted an area outside to plant flowers, though—especially roses.

The Waters had been married 42 years and had four grown children and seven grandchildren. They had been entertaining family for years, but with grandchildren, they found themselves enjoying going to their kids' homes for family events rather than hosting them. They also liked having their grandkids overnight when possible.

As Luther approached retirement, they decided it was time to sell their four-bedroom family home and move into something with less upkeep, so they talked to their children about selling the family home. Their kids had mixed emotions about it, but overall, they wanted what was best for their parents and supported their decision.

Luther and Danita were excited to find a townhome just a few miles from their youngest daughter. It had a two-car garage and a small yard that allowed both Luther and Danita to continue the hobbies they loved but with far less maintenance. The two bedrooms meant they could still have the grandkids over, and there was a park within walking distance that they could all enjoy together.

Danita had heard about reverse mortgage loans, but she was unsure how that would work for them since they were just downsizing. Their home was paid off, so they knew that once they sold it, they would be able to buy their new townhome outright. However, when talking to their reverse mortgage planner, instead of buying the home outright, they learned they could use a reverse mortgage loan in conjunction with the purchase of their new townhome. This allowed them to keep more than half of the proceeds from the sale of their home for retirement needs and put less money down to purchase the townhome. They also had a line of credit available to them if needed.

Reverse mortgage loan proceeds are usually tax-free, unlike Danita's income. The money they had put away for retirement seemed like enough, but it would cause them to live more frugally, and they both had concerns about outliving their income, as they were both active and healthy. They felt that having the reverse mortgage funds available as a line of credit helped them by allowing them to access funds without fear when unexpected expenses arose. And with grandchildren to enjoy, they never knew when they might need some extra money!

THE MEYERS PAID OFF THEIR MORTGAGE AND CREDIT CARDS...AND TOOK A TRIP

David and Michelle met later in life, both divorcees with grown children. Michelle was an interior designer, something that became quickly evident when walking into their quaint home. David was a truck driver and loved to tell stories about the America he had seen over the years. Michelle continued to do some interior design work and also enjoyed volunteering. She liked to visit her son and daughter's families every year, both of which lived out of state. David's children lived nearby, and he enjoyed watching his grandkids play sports on the weekends.

At ages 71 and 66, the Meyers were a few years into retirement when their furnace went out, costing them several thousand dollars to replace. A bad storm also caused damage to their roof, and while insurance covered the roof, they still had to pay a large deductible. These unexpected expenses caused the Meyers to tighten their budget's belt. They were still doing okay, but it made them consider what they'd do if something else were to go wrong. They believed they would cross that bridge when they came to it.

Then, something exciting happened. David's cousin reached out to him and invited him to attend their family reunion—the first in a decade. They really wanted to attend, but with their limited budget, they didn't know how they could. Michelle felt the reunion was important, as it would likely be the last time they would see certain family members. She wanted the vacation and wanted to get to know more of the family members she had not yet met, but whom David had talked so much about.

They sat down together to look at their budget and how to make the reunion possible. David reluctantly brought up the idea of a reverse mortgage. Michelle said she didn't know much about them but was open to getting the facts if it meant they could take the trip.

David and Michelle met with a reverse mortgage planner, who explained how the process worked and how they could receive and use the equity from their home, usually tax-free. The advisor answered their questions, and they were surprised how recent changes to reverse mortgages made it a viable option for them. They reworked their budget and saw that not only could they eliminate their mortgage, but they could also pay off a high-interest credit card, reducing their monthly expenses so they could put money aside for any future emergencies. They also discovered that they could take some money to travel to the reunion.

David described the experience as being similar to reaching into the pocket of an old coat and finding cash. He never thought that using his home's equity could help them in this way. David's children decided to join him on the trip for the family reunion. It was a great experience that also allowed his children to connect with extended family, something he feels is a true legacy.

THE BARKERS GO THEIR SEPARATE WAYS, AND EACH GETS A HOME

 Ron and Linda Barker had been married for 36 years but had recently grown apart. With their children grown and living on their own, Ron and Linda discovered they didn't have much in common any longer. Now in their early 60s, they decided to each go their separate ways.

As they met with their divorce attorneys to divide up the assets, they began to understand that their home, which they owned free and clear, may be able to benefit both of them. Linda wanted to keep their $400,000 home and was willing to get a reverse mortgage, taking out $200,000 to give to Ron for his half of the equity.

Linda was thrilled that she wouldn't have a mortgage payment as long as she paid the property taxes, homeowners insurance, maintained the home, and lived in it at least six months or more a year—all of which she was willing to do. Linda was blown away that this was even possible.

Ron benefitted by taking his $200,000 equity stake and buying a maintenance-free patio home for $300,000, with only $150,000 down. He, too, will never have a mortgage payment, as he bought his patio home using a reverse mortgage. Ron was thrilled to have $50,000 left over to provide updates on the home and keep an emergency fund if needed.

The only person the Barkers appreciated more than the divorce attorney who introduced them to their reverse mortgage planner, was the reverse mortgage planner himself, who made it all come together in a timely fashion.

BETSY LUNDEN FIXED HER HOME—AND HER HEART

 Betsy was widowed at 71. She and her late husband, Keith, had celebrated their 50-year anniversary just before his passing. She appreciated when their three children, who all lived out of state, would come to visit, but it never felt like enough. As much as she wanted to have company, she rarely felt like leaving the house for social events. Her kids had encouraged her to get out, but she just didn't feel like she had the energy for much more than heading to church once a week. She had a neighbor come weekly to help with chores, and that seemed to be working.

However, greater plans were in the works. It was at a church function that she met Gary Kline. He invited her to a luncheon for a nonprofit, where he served on the board of directors. Gary, also a widower, had a comfortable retirement financially but wanted a partner with whom to spend time.

Gary and Betsy enjoyed each other's company and began having dinner together, which eventually turned toward romance. They decided to date, and Betsy was very happy to have someone in her life again. However, as time went on, Gary saw Betsy's need for a new roof and porch and minor outdoor repairs, which he offered to pay for. Betsy decided to tap the home equity she had built up over the years and use a reverse mortgage to access the equity. She wanted Gary to be able to reap the rewards of his savings without worry and also be able to continue to serve the nonprofit he was passionate about.

Betsy said that meeting Gary helped her to start living again, and fixing the house became a metaphor for fixing her heart. They had many things in common, including a love of cheesecake! Once a month after church, they enjoy a piece of cheesecake with sliced strawberries and celebrate the next phase of their lives. The reverse mortgage funds helped Betsy to feel empowered to get her life back, and she's doing it.

CASH
FLOW

SALLY ATCHISON FREED UP $1,000 A MONTH

Sally Atchison, age 74 and a former RN, always considered herself independent. As a single mom, she felt she had learned how to manage well that way. And, as a nurse, she always took care of others but had also learned a balance that allowed her to take care of herself. Whether taking a water aerobics class, walking her dog 2.3 miles around the lake, or visiting the library for the newest crime novel, she enjoyed spending her retirement in ways that nurtured her.

However, living purely on Social Security, she found it difficult to meet her monthly obligations with the rising cost of living. When she began using a credit card to purchase groceries, her daughter Jennifer saw the statement and questioned her about it. Sally was still making a mortgage payment in addition to the credit card bill, and Jennifer wasn't in a financial position to help.

Jennifer had heard of reverse mortgages and asked her mom if they could meet with a professional to get more information. The reverse mortgage planner explained the process and the impact it would have on Sally's budget. To the women's surprise, Sally could free up nearly $1,000 a month by paying off her mortgage and credit cards with the reverse mortgage, while also being able to stay in her home, something the independent Sally valued highly. Jennifer was relieved to know she wouldn't inherit her mom's debt.

A reverse mortgage is a non-recourse loan, where the house owes the mortgage, not a person. Jennifer also didn't need to worry about her mom being able to cover her daily expenses. Every Monday, Jennifer now goes to Sally's house to help with chores and enjoy lunch with her mother. When Jennifer sets the groceries on the kitchen table, she feels a sense of gratitude for the opportunity her mom had to use the equity in her home to keep her there. It seemed perfectly serendipitous that the home Sally had invested in caring for all these years was now caring for her.

THE XIAOS EXTENDED THEIR RETIREMENT CASH FLOW

 Chen and Ling Xiao had longevity in their blood. Parents on both sides of their family had lived into their 90s. In fact, Ling's grandmother lived to be 101. With good health at ages 72 and 70, respectively, the Xaios were concerned about outliving their retirement savings. Chen had worked in manufacturing, creating valves and piping for industrial and commercial use. He attributes good eating and an active lifestyle to his health. Ling had worked since she was a teen, but said her favorite position of all time was working as a vet tech. She appreciated how animals always seem to trust, love, and connect on a different level than humans. She attributed her good health to happiness and good genes.

The Xiaos met each other at a very young age, and they both described their relationship as happy—something that very possibly also aided in their longevity. They were rarely seen apart from each other and kept an immaculate yard and home. Even though their home was over 100 years old, they had owned it for 35 of those years, keeping it in top condition. They hoped to stay there forever.

With no mortgage payment, their expenses were low, but inflation continued to rise, and their money in savings wasn't stretching as far as it used to even a few years ago. They hoped that their son would one day take care of them, but a divorce had caused him financial difficulty, and he was still paying back student loans. The Xiaos wanted a financial tool that would help extend the life of the assets they had built up.

Chen's older brother, Joon, was a lawyer with a very large home and no children. He told them that they may be able to position the equity in their home in a way that would extend the life of their retirement funds by allowing them to delay having to tap into them. By choosing a reverse mortgage they could stay in their home while also allowing their investments to increase. Joon mentioned that he recently had a client go through that process and was very happy with the outcome.

The Xiaos weren't sure how reverse mortgages worked, which made them nervous, but they decided to become educated about the process and brought a lot of questions to their reverse mortgage planner. Through that process, the skepticism was reduced, and their misconception that the lender would own their home was corrected. They decided to take a small lump sum to make a few minor repairs and modifications to their home, and then receive monthly cash flow tax-free instead of using their retirement savings.

This strategy afforded them several more years of increased cash flow they hadn't previously considered. They were very satisfied with their decision and now look forward to many more years together in their home.

THE SANDOVALS WIPED OUT THEIR CREDIT CARD DEBT

 Bill Sandoval loved that he was able to be the breadwinner, allowing his wife, Nancy, to stay home and take care of their children. It was especially important when John, their second child, was born with Down's Syndrome. Nancy was able to stay home with him and his older sister, Sarah, and provide care to both of them. Sarah was now a special education teacher in Pennsylvania, and John had passed away at only 37 due to complications related to his condition. The loss took both an emotional and financial toll on the couple, but they both kept a positive outlook and were thankful for all they had.

Nancy now volunteered with the Special Olympics, an organization she had been part of when John was alive. It brought her joy and comfort after their loss. Bill and Nancy, at 67 and 62, respectively, had done their best to put money aside for retirement but felt they were short of the full savings they desired. Bill wanted to retire but wasn't sure how they would afford to keep their lifestyle, which was already frugal. Their credit card debt had been growing over the years, as they used it to help cover expenses when a large chunk of income went to covering John's care and expenses that health insurance didn't cover. The Sandovals also used debt to pay for a much-needed family vacation before Sarah left home.

It was Nancy who brought up the idea of a reverse mortgage. Their son-in-law, Frank, was a reverse mortgage planner and had explained how the laws had changed regarding Home Equity Mortgage Conversion (HEMC) and that it may be a good option for them. Sarah and Frank were settled in State College and wanted Bill and Nancy to be able to enjoy their retirement years. Frank explained to them how the reverse mortgage could be used to eliminate their debt, freeing up just over $500 a month. They were also able to have a small line of credit available to them in case any other unexpected expenses arose. It would allow Bill to retire and have a safety net.

Bill and Nancy looked at other options but came back to the reverse mortgage as the best option for them. They compared the costs of the reverse mortgage to the interest they were paying on the credit cards, and they loved the idea of having a safety net so they didn't have to create even more credit card debt in the case of an emergency.

Bill now volunteers with Nancy at the Special Olympics. His favorite part is putting the medals around the participants' necks. His fear of not being able to retire with enough money was eased by leveraging the equity in his home to free them from years of debt.

THE THOMPSONS DELAYED COLLECTING SOCIAL SECURITY

Joe and Jada Thompson had been married 50 years and were pleasantly surprised when their two children threw them a surprise anniversary party. The pictures from the event sat on their coffee table in a book their oldest daughter put together for them. Of course, next to that was an album of pictures of their five grandchildren.

The Thompsons had married at ages 19 and 18, having met in high school. "I was aware of Joe and would watch him run track," remembers Jada, "but we never dated. The last day of senior year, we were at a party to celebrate the end of school. He walked over to me and introduced himself." Jada smiled and looked at him. "He has the brightest eyes."

Joe looked at her confidently. He spent his entire career in sales, but what he sold changed through the years— everything from hardware to lighting fixtures to office supplies. Jada made a living as a receptionist in the dental field after their kids started school. Five years ago, when Joe was ready to retire, his certified financial planner brought up the idea of using a reverse mortgage to leverage their home equity and delay collecting on Social Security benefits.

"I hadn't heard anything good about reverse mortgages," Joe admitted. "I only thought they caused people to lose their homes. The advisor explained that waiting until we were 70 years old to collect on our Social Security benefits would be very advantageous to us. I was skeptical, but he showed me what the benefits were and how they compared to the increased income. It just made sense."

Joe had put money aside for retirement and felt confident about their insurance and savings. He never considered using his home's equity, assuming he would leave it to his kids after he and Jada passed. Instead, he increased his life insurance amount so his children would receive more money tax-free. It was an important decision, and one that allowed them more financial freedom, so they took advantage of it.

The changes to the guidelines in reverse mortgages allowed the Thompsons to use their home, one of their largest assets, to extend the life of their retirement savings. Once their Social Security benefits were being drawn on, they chose the option to have their reverse mortgage funding as a line of credit to use for any unexpected expenses. Because the funds were tax-free, they were able to keep their investments building value without pulling money out of them, giving the Thompsons additional peace of mind.

THE COLES SUPPLEMENTED THEIR CASH FLOW

 Tim and Cathy Cole said they should have known they would be married the day Tim's family moved into the neighborhood 50 years ago. But, they didn't end up dating each other until they had both returned from their first year of college. Tim went to school in Nebraska, while Cathy attended college in California. Their parents had become friends in addition to being neighbors. Tim and Cathy were at a family BBQ when they became reacquainted. Of course, they knew each other in high school, but were in different crowds and didn't really spend much time together.

Tim had gone to school for environmental sciences, and Cathy was hoping to go into human resources. They began dating, and shortly thereafter, got married and welcomed three children, all sons: Noah, Caleb, and David. Cathy stayed home to raise the boys and support them with their extracurricular activities, which were sports for Jacob, photography for Caleb, and art for David.

Cathy also began taking up photography as a hobby that eventually turned into a part-time career. After the boys were out of the house, Tim's job relocated him to California, and at ages 56 and 54, the Coles began calling California their new home. Eight years after their relocation, however, Tim was laid off and found himself needing employment—not an easy situation to be in.

He had several interviews and was being told he was over-qualified, which to him meant that he wanted more money that what they wanted to offer. He considered his options and chose a position that offered less money but good benefits and a short commute. It put a strain on their day-to-day expenses, as he still wanted to contribute to his retirement accounts so they wouldn't outlive their money.

One day while golfing, Tim was talking to his long-time friend, James, who had recently used a reverse mortgage to downsize. Tim was surprised to hear about James's choice and asked if he was worried about losing his house if the lender sold it out from under him. James, a CPA, explained that he still owns all the rights to his house and that the new HECM rules were designed to help seniors in retirement, not hurt them. He encouraged Tim to speak to the reverse mortgage planner he had used.

Tim and Cathy met with the reverse mortgage planner and discovered that they could qualify for a reverse mortgage. Additionally, they had several options on how to use the funds, including receiving a monthly payment, just like a part-time income, but tax-free. Tim realized the increased cash flow would make up for his pay decrease and help them make their bills easier to manage. Not only did it eliminate their mortgage payment, saving them money, but it gave them a little extra cash each month.

Cathy continues to take photography, mostly as a hobby, and Tim continues to work, neither giving up a single thing they love.

THE IVANOVS LET THEIR INVESTMENTS GROW

The Ivanovs saw much of their wealth disappear in the last economic dip. It extended Alexander's need to keep working at the body shop, rather than retiring. He had transitioned from performing repairs to front desk management about three years ago at age 62. His tough exterior hid the fact that his body didn't want to manage the physical component of his job anymore. Behind the desk, he made less money but found it surprisingly fulfilling to estimate repairs and talk to the customers about the reason they came in to see him, whether that was hitting a pothole, hail damage, or backing into a dumpster. He would've preferred to retire last year, but a few more years of working behind a desk "weren't going to kill him," as he phrased it. He still found time on the weekends to go fishing with his two best friends.

Helena worked as a beautician, and the only things that made her happier than her job were her daughters. Her youngest just re-married, and her oldest had given her a grandson, who would be starting school in the fall. At age 59, she still loved going dancing and going on motorcycle rides on sunny weekends with her husband. She was worried about how the economy was affecting their retirement funds, as well as the impact it was having on Alexander's psyche.

A favorite client, Sue, told Helena that she and her husband had used their home equity through a reverse mortgage to help pay for some expenses. Helena wondered if they could benefit from a reverse mortgage as well, and asked Sue for the name of her reverse mortgage planner. They scheduled to meet with her and get more information about the new HECM program and how it worked. The Ivanovs say it's the best decision they ever made.

The Ivanovs were able to take a reverse mortgage that allowed them to get increased cash flow to help cover expenses when Alexander was ready to retire. He was glad to know he could keep his investments recovering while having tax-free cash flow entering their household. It gave him peace of mind, knowing that his investments would grow over the next few years while he and Helena were still able to work. Alexander found it easier to go to work with the freedom to retire, even though he wasn't ready yet.

In the future, weekends riding his motorcycle with his wife or fishing with friends would be something he could choose to do any day, but for now, he was willing to wait, knowing the retirement funds he worked so hard to build would be able to mature and grow.

THE DUGAS HAVE A CASH RESERVE

Chris Duga thought he would never retire. His wife, Lily, wondered the same thing. Chris had taken a job at a nearby grocery store after his official retirement from his job as a plant manager. Lily said Chris was never good with money, spending it lavishly to have the things he wanted in life. Chris admits that he lived as though he'd never reach retirement. He jokes that he still doesn't believe it's here. His small savings would likely not stretch very far, but he felt fortunate to have paid off his mortgage early and still feel able bodied and sharp minded enough to work. Lily said Chris had the energy of someone 15 years younger, and while she supported his desire to continue to work, she did miss the idea of having someone to travel with in their retirementyears.

Lily had always been the frugal one, storing away quite a bit of her income as an administrative assistant for their retirement. Chris still felt it was his job to provide income, but that was becoming more difficult as their house aged right alongside them. They decided it was time to downsize, so they sold their home for maintenance-free living in an active adult condominium complex where a few of their friends lived.

Most days, Chris would go to work, while Lily headed poolside or took a weekend retreat with her girlfriends, leaving him behind. Finally, one day, Chris decided he was ready to have a more leisurely life, one like his wife had. With the sale of their house and reduction of their bills, he felt he could, but he wanted to meet first with his financial advisor to be sure.

Andy, his financial advisor, told Chris that he could retire, but he would have a strict budget to manage, something he knew Chris struggled with. He brought up the benefits that a reverse mortgage could afford them, specifically a standby cash reserve for irregular bills. Together, they worked out a budget, allowing for some flex spending for both Chris and Lily, as well as a cash savings for things out of the ordinary.

Andy suggested to them that Lily be the one to manage the cash reserve, and together they playfully agreed that Chris could only access the money with both Lily and Andy's approval. It was the hardest Chris had laughed in quite some time. He was looking forward to spending time with his wife and finally being retired. And Lily was thrilled to have a travel companion.

MEDICAL

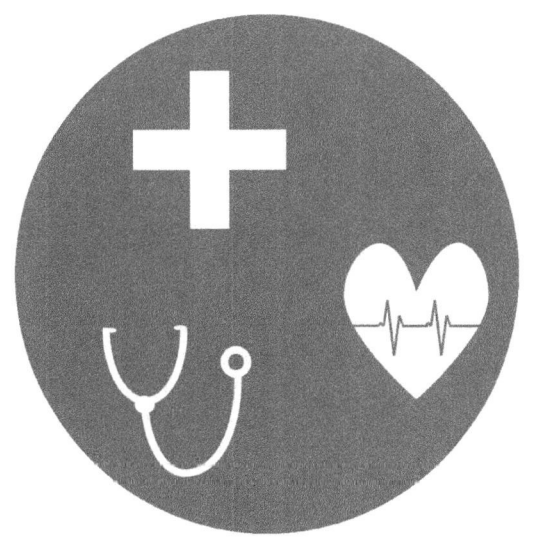

THE RAMKISSOONS PAID FOR MEDICAL CARE

 Ban Ramkissoon spent years as a business consultant for a well-known national corporation, while his wife, Yashvi, as a childcare provider, surrounded herself with children, which were her passion. Their own two children were grown and were busy professionals, and the Ramkissoons were happily working and building their retirement funds.

After a persistent cough wouldn't seem to lighten up, Ban decided to see a doctor. His cancer diagnosis was something that shocked the entire family. Over the next six months, the Ramkissoons met with doctor after doctor to find solutions, and a year later they found themselves several hundred thousand dollars in medical and credit card debt.

Yashvi had dropped to part-time work to help care for Ban, and they hired skilled nursing to provide additional support in his recovery. While Ban was undergoing chemotherapy, he physically didn't feel well enough to work. Without full-time employment, the family income dropped dramatically, while the use of credit cards increased. Although Ban's cancer was treated, and he began feeling better, the couple felt as though they were starting all over with their finances while only in their early 60s. It was certainly not at all what they had planned for.

Foreclosure became a very real possibility, and they knew they needed help. They'd always wanted to leave their home to their children but realized now that was no longer likely. The Ramkissoons didn't want to leave their home. In fact, when they purchased it, they did so strategically to be able to live there the rest of their lives. The home was still very useful to them, and the thought of moving was troublesome.

Frantically, Yashvi began researching options to save their home. In the process, they learned about reverse mortgages. They came to understand that sometimes plans change in unforeseen ways. If they went into foreclosure, they would have nothing to leave their children, but with a reverse mortgage, they could keep their home. It seemed like their best option. Although it wasn't what they were planning on, they were thankful they had a reverse mortgage option available.

Through their experience, they realized the value of health and living each day to the fullest. They learned the value of acquiring information and help and being able to use the resources they had built when they were younger to get them through a tough time now. Obtaining a reverse mortgage helped them pay their medical bills, remain in their home, and never have a mortgage payment as long as they paid the taxes and insurance, and maintained the home.

THE KNIGHTS PAID THEIR MEDICARE PART C AND D COSTS

Larry Knight and his wife, Robin, both age 65, met as teenagers when they worked at the same grocery store. Larry said that he had liked Robin since he first saw her. After dating for two years, they got married, and over the following decade, had three children. They moved around a lot as a young family, and it wasn't until later in life when they settled down that Larry secured a stable job as a cable installer.

It was then that they bought their first home. They were close to paying it off as Larry entered retirement. Robin had mostly been a stay-at-home mom, but after their children left home she had taken part-time work helping seniors with various tasks. Through that process, she realized the value of Medicare and the benefits it provides, especially given Larry's need for medications related to his blood pressure and cholesterol.

With Larry's income ending and a large house payment to come up with each month, they were concerned with how they would manage expenses when their group health insurance coverage ended and Medicare kicked in. Larry had been told about reverse mortgages from his boss, Bob, but didn't think one would work for him because he didn't own his home free and clear. Nonetheless, Bob gave Larry the contact details for the reverse mortgage planner that he himself had worked with.

Robin admitted she was frustrated and skeptical about the idea when Larry first proposed it to her, but after talking with the reverse mortgage planner and learning about the new rules and regulations, it made more sense to them. Even though their house wasn't completely paid off, they had built up enough equity that they could use a reverse mortgage to eliminate their mortgage payments in retirement, as well as help offset their health care costs with Medicare Parts C and D. The reverse mortgage solution would free up several hundred dollars per month.

The Knights had assumed they wouldn't qualify for a reverse mortgage and had resigned themselves to the idea that they'd likely be working well into their retirement years until their mortgage was paid off. They were relieved to see that they had another option. Ironically, they both decided to take on part-time work, and they chose work that was more enjoyable to them.

Robin is now working at a nonprofit that she believes in, helping with administrative tasks a few times a week. Larry took a part-time position at a hardware store, something he had always wanted to do to get a discount on home improvement products. He fully takes advantage of the employee discount to work on some of the "honey-do" projects he has around the house.

THE LEES PURCHASED A LONG-TERM CARE POLICY

Paul and Stacey Lee, ages 68 and 69, respectively, sat across from their financial planner. It was a cool fall day, almost a year to the day from Paul's retirement as a career deliveryman and supervisor. Stacey had been a homemaker, taking odd jobs and volunteer opportunities as her interests directed her. About six months ago, Paul had made his final mortgage payment, and the Lees celebrated with a second honeymoon to Hawaii. They were concerned that their financial advisor would tell them the vacation had been a bad idea, and they would get a stern finger wagging. He had done this in the past, typically in a playful manner.

"Did you get any good pictures?" Herbert, their financial planner, asked flatly. The Lees nodded, and Herbert laughed, breaking the tension. Paul and Stacey shared stories about the freshness of the islands' pineapple and the macadamia nut factory they visited. Herbert had been to Hawaii with his wife and congratulated them on taking the time to get away. The conversation became a bit more serious as Herbert began asking questions to review the couple's goals into their retirement.

Herbert asked several questions about their health and suggested that they consider investing in a long-term care insurance policy. Because they were both still healthy, he felt it would be a good idea for them to spend money on a long-term care policy while it was still fairly affordable. They had declined taking a policy when they were younger, but the ability to qualify now would help them well into the next decade, despite the higher premium. Herbert also suggested that instead of creating a financial hit to their monthly budget, which they were managing well, that they take a reverse mortgage and use the tax-free funds to pay for the premium payment each month.

The Lees were surprised by the suggestion. They had been so excited to have a debt and mortgage-free retirement, and they were afraid of losing their house to the lender. They also had a concern about how they would pay for long-term care, knowing it could bankrupt them if either of them needed it. They didn't want to outlive their retirement funds, but they didn't want to have huge debt in the future either.

Herbert explained the new rules and safety precautions that were included in the new HECM reverse mortgage. They wouldn't lose their home or pass the mortgage debt onto their children, as the house owes the money, not the borrowers or their heirs. The equity in their home would be used to pay their long-term care premiums, so they'd have coverage when they needed it, and it would allow one or both of them to stay in the home rather than sell it if they needed care.

Paul and Stacey considered Herbert's advice, and they decided to take it. Not only did it give them peace of mind, knowing that their long-term needs would be covered, but they could now have a small line of cash available to them in case of an emergency, rather than tapping into their retirement funds.

After years of paying on their home, they never considered that their home could pay them. Paul wondered if it was worth another honeymoon to celebrate the reverse mortgage!

JOHN O'HARE FILLED THE MEDICARE GAP

John O'Hare loved traveling to other states for art fairs, where he was able to show his handcrafted pottery pieces. An artist his whole life, only recently did he pursue his art full-time in his retirement. His simple home offered him the perfect work space that allowed him to make his creations—and a big mess! Clay was nearly everywhere. The irony is that he had worked the last ten years in a janitorial company, where he was responsible for keeping everything clean. Prior to that, he'd worked odd jobs but still always produced the beautiful pottery, which would now be his only project in retirement.

The biggest problem John faced was that of his health insurance expense. At age 62, he wasn't yet eligible for Medicare, and the monthly premiums were difficult to manage, yet required, due to his diabetes.

John's home was paid for, and he appreciated not having a mortgage payment. But, with his irregular income, he was concerned about losing his health insurance due to nonpayment and wanted another option. He talked to his best friend, Bill, about the option of a reverse mortgage. He had heard of these mortgages but didn't know much about them. Bill explained that he and his wife were skeptical about them as well but learned with the new regulations that they were a helpful option.

With that advice, John decided to contact a reverse mortgage planner and learn more. He was pleased to discover that he could use a reverse mortgage to help pay his health insurance premiums until he was Medicare eligible. And after that, he could continue to use the proceeds to help offset costs associated with Medicare Part D for his diabetes supplies. He was also pleased to learn that as long as he paid his property taxes, homeowners insurance, and maintained the home, he could stay in his house as long as he was able. John received a great deal of peace of mind and satisfaction in knowing that he could continue his retirement hobby, including traveling, without the worry of medical insurance lapses.

Reverse mortgage options may not be the best option for everyone, or for every situation, but in John's case, it gave him peace of mind that helped him enjoy his retirement years. He truly believes that he doesn't need to be a starving artist. In fact, he handcrafts plates and bowls that others use at their dinner tables. And when he gets home, he has all he needs to fire up his kiln and create his next masterpiece.

THE LIPSONS PAID FOR A MEDICAL EMERGENCY

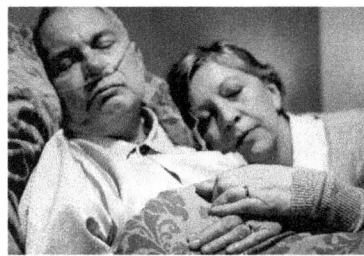 Jason Lipson never expected to have a heart attack at age 57. In the five years since then, he had taken care of himself by eating better and taking walks with his wife, Loretta. Loretta still worries about Jason but was thankful for the wake-up call that caused him to make healthier choices, even though he was still a smoker. His career as an HVAC technician had ended early, and she was thankful that she was still able to work managing a retail clothing store at age 63. Neither of them expected that on the way home from work late one night, she'd end up in a car accident, hit by a drunk driver who ran a stoplight.

The medical bills, while covered by insurance, still held a several thousand-dollar deductible along with the co-pay amount. The lawsuit she opened wouldn't pay out for quite some time, and without her income, they were struggling to make their house payment. The attorney suggested that Loretta consider a temporary income source and encouraged her to look at the option of a reverse mortgage.

The Lipsons were skeptical as to how a reverse mortgage could help them in their situation, but they met with a reverse mortgage planner anyway. He helped them see how a lump sum payment from their home equity could help meet their current financial needs to keep them above water until they could get back on their feet.

They agreed with the plan, and Jason took on part-time work to add additional income to the family. Loretta was able to recover and return to work, and the settlement money came in, nearly 18 months later. They used the reverse mortgage funds to pay off an installment loan and eliminate their mortgage payment, as well as stop some medical bills from going to collections.

From the settlement, they were able to put money back into their savings, and Jason was able to retire, again. This time, Loretta joined him. They now have the remaining home equity from the reverse mortgage as a line of credit for them to draw on and only use in the case of an emergency, which thankfully, they haven't had. Jason and Loretta decided to add an adopted dog to their family so they can continue their walks at the park, and to continue taking care of their health for years to come.

THE LOMBARDIS PAID FOR LONG-TERM CARE NEED

Phil Lombardi came from a long line of blue-collar tradesman; his father and grandfather were both carpenters. Phil decided to go into construction and jokes that, after 45 years, he really is a Jack of All Trades, skilled in nearly all the trades that go into home building.

His wife, Sandy, an early education teacher, is 62. Phil is 70 and suffered a stroke at age 66. Sandy and Phil used to walk around the park every Saturday morning after he retired. He would frequently look at the homes and tell Sandy stories of houses he built as they passed the homes in the neighborhood. But none were as great as the home he'd built for him and his wife. It was Sandy's dream home. They had a small garden in the back of the house, as well as a small chicken coop, and three goats.

When Phil had his stroke, Sandy was afraid she was going to lose him. He had life insurance in place, but they hadn't put anything in place for long-term care, and the stroke caused Phil to need care that Sandy physically couldn't handle alone. She needed help bathing Phil and getting him to and from doctors' appointments. Sandy considered early retirement to help, but had two more years before she could claim her full pension. She decided it was better to continue working.

She was worried about the financial impact of the stroke and decided to meet with their financial advisor, who offered her and Phil several options, including looking at a reverse mortgage. He referred them to a reverse mortgage planner to analyze their needs and goals to determine if it was a good step for the couple to take.

The new regulations with reverse mortgage allowed them to choose several methods for receiving the equity from their home. They took a small lump sum to pay off debts from the stroke and then opted for small, monthly, tax-free payments to pay for Phil's long-term care needs.

[*"According to the U.S. Department of Health and Human Services, about 70% of people turning 65 will need long-term care services at some point in their lives."* SOURCE: www.longtermcare.gov/the-basics September 2013]

DREAM

THE ROMANS WANTED A LINE OF CREDIT FOR THEIR BUSINESS

Jerry and Lisa always dreamt of having a restaurant in their retirement, so when the small coffee shop in their town came up for sale, they jumped right on it. The coffee shop had been quite busy for years, but the owners decided to move out of state and wanted to sell it. The Romans knew that using some of their retirement income was potentially risky, but they had planned for an opportunity such as this.

After a year of owning the shop, they'd spent a significant portion of their retirement, and it was starting to pay off. They were paying their bills and replenishing their retirement accounts. However, they were afraid that the income wasn't coming in fast enough, and if they hit a bump in the road, they could lose not only the business but their life savings.

They considered a business line of credit but didn't have enough small business experience. Then they learned about the reverse mortgage line of credit they could get by obtaining a reverse mortgage. A traditional home equity line of credit would require them to qualify based on their credit score and have them pay the loan back with interest and principal. They also ran the risk of the HELOC being frozen, closed, or the loan amount being reduced.

The HECM line of credit, however, would allow them to use the equity they had already paid into their home as a tax-free funding source. There'd be no payments due to the lender until they moved out. This was also a way for them to protect their equity against any market corrections. It sounded too good to be true, so they met with a reverse mortgage planner to ask questions about how it worked and how it could be used.

The Romans were concerned with losing their home to the lender, but the reverse mortgage planner explained that as long as they lived in the home and continued to pay the taxes, insurance, and maintain the house as they always had, they wouldn't lose their home. He also explained that the loan was based on the appraised value of the home, and their home equity would be protected, despite what happens in the real estate market.

Jerry and Lisa saw the reverse mortgage line of credit as a cushion in case of an emergency while they continued to run their coffee shop. They updated the signage, which was something they had wanted to do but were afraid to spend money for, until they had the reverse mortgage funds. It was a good investment because the new signs brought new customers into the restaurant, and business increased.

Today, Jerry and Lisa are proud of their accomplishment and the realization of their dream. As nerve-racking as the risk was, they'll say it was worth it to have something to work on together as business owners and to continue the coffee shop's legacy in their town.

JOSEPHINE MONTGOMERY WANTED TO SEE MORE OF THE USA

Josephine Montgomery's parents had immigrated to the United States when she was just two years old, and her brothers were five and six. Her father, a produce farmer, found restaurant kitchen work and then worked his way into better positions. From his success, he opened his own small bar and restaurant while Josie was still in high school.

Josie married and divorced young, with two small children. When she remarried at age 36, she and her new husband, Walter, were both on their second marriages. Their relationship had been rocky since the beginning, and after the death of his mother, Walter spiraled deeply into alcoholism, which lead to a fatal accident. Without a life insurance policy, Josephine was devastated emotionally and financially.

In her grief, she found herself in physical pain and sought relief by receiving her first professional massage. The massage itself was wonderful, but she described it as a 'God moment,' as the massages triggered the decision to throw herself into massage therapy school.

She had been working as a waitress, and she loved the interaction with others, but she found massage therapy to be her passion. She believed massage school was the best decision she had ever made, and at age 63, she owned her home and had put her two children through school. Her son, Rodney, was a chef in Las Vegas, and her daughter, Michelle, ran a day care center in Arizona. While the kids grew up, Josie used her home as both a massage studio and her family's residence, and now she wanted to pull some of the equity out of it to make a very special purchase: a travel trailer.

Josephine considered selling her home but wanted something to come back to when she was ready. A neighbor agreed to keep her home up while Josie was away. She had been shopping for travel trailers for quite a while, waiting for the time when she'd retire and get to see all of what the United States has to offer.

Josie realized that her home was one of her biggest assets and rather than sell, she decided to keep it and enjoy the appreciation it offered. Since she travelled some, she didn't want the burden of a mortgage payment. The funeral director for Walter's ceremony suggested she look into a reverse mortgage. After meeting with a local, licensed Reverse Mortgage Planner, she was able to eliminate her monthly payment and have a line of credit available when needed. An added bonus is the line of credit grows at least 5% a year with compound interest!

Even as a young girl, Josie wished she could visit the many places and tourist spots on the map; something her family never had the luxury of doing. In her retirement, and with the help of a reverse mortgage, her American dream was finally coming true. Besides massage therapy, it's the happiest Josie has ever been.

THE WALSHES FUNDED THEIR PASSION

Geoff and Sarah Walsh had two more years of mortgage payments. In their mid-70s, they felt relatively healthy and vibrant but not healthy enough to go on their church's missions trip, which they were passionate about. They had served as missionaries in the past; in fact, that's how they met. They saw devotion in each other in the service they performed, and it became a regular part of their giving through the 53 years they've been together. They never had children of their own, and their missions became the thing that brought them closer and kept them busy. They discussed other ways they could support the missions team and how they could give more to charity overall.

The Walshes had life insurance policies that would benefit each other when needed, and they had also named a charity as a beneficiary. However, they knew they'd never see the fruit of that gift and wanted to make an impact while they were still living. They spoke to their CPA, who suggested they take a look at a reverse mortgage to meet their gift-giving goal.

Geoff and Sarah discovered that, by using a reverse mortgage and leveraging the equity in their home, they could eliminate the last two years of their mortgage payment. Not only did this increase their monthly cash flow, but it allowed them to have additional funds available, which permitted them to stay in their home longer. The Walshes decided that in lieu of making a full mortgage payment each month, they would take 50 percent of their former mortgage payment and send it to a missionary instead.

This was the impact they wanted to have, and they knew how beneficial their money would be overseas in the hands of a missionary. They recalled how much their faith had grown to see God provide for them and how far they could stretch their small income when they had served decades before. They chose to support a missionary from their church—a 22-year-old young man with a passion to translate the New Testament for distribution in areas where people didn't have access to the Bible.

Although they couldn't go on the missions trip physically, they felt as though they sent their hearts along with the team. They were thankful that both in life and in their passing they could make a contribution to their passion.

JOSEPH PEREZ BECAME AN ENTREPRENEUR

 Sixty-two-year-old Joseph Perez had spent the last 15 years with the same company as a systems analyst before he was laid off in July. But the idea of retirement wasn't on his mind for at least another five to ten years. He loved his job because he loved being a problem solver, and he felt that his job kept his mind sharp. With this layoff however, he considered working part-time rather than full-time, but he knew that to make the money he wanted, he'd likely need to continue working full-time for five more years to build his retirement account.

As Joseph began looking for work, he found it increasingly frustrating to find a position that would satisfy both his financial means and give him more time to enjoy his hobbies of model railroading and golf. He decided instead to become an entrepreneur—a freelancer—offering business and system analysis for small business owners. This was something new for him, and he was concerned about tapping into his savings in order to pay himself until his business could get off the ground. He'd been using the same tax accountant for several years and asked for some advice.

His CPA encouraged Joseph to speak to a trusted mortgage planner he knew who provided reverse mortgage options. The planner reviewed the recent changes with Joseph, explaining how fees, options to access his equity, and requirements worked in regard to reverse mortgages.

For Joseph, the tax-free proceeds provided by the reverse mortgage would give him the opportunity to have the necessary money to create and run his new business venture. It was an ideal situation, where he could use his experience and knowledge to help others in a way that provided him the financial security to not be laid off again.

Joseph was able to choose an option that allowed a larger lump sum and smaller proceeds as his business grew. He now has the option to retire if and when he's ready, and to pick up a game of golf as it suits him.

Joseph had never considered using the equity in his home to give him the freedom he now had by being his own boss. It was as though at age 62, he had finally realized the true American dream.

SARAH SNYDER HELD ONTO HER ASSETS AND LEFT A LEGACY

Sarah Snyder was 72 years old. A retired paralegal, she had lost her husband, James, last year. His life insurance paid off the house and allowed for final expenses to be covered, but her day-to-day income was from Social Security benefits, which were getting tighter and tighter. James had put away some money for retirement and had invested in gold coins and art work that he intended to sell in retirement for additional income. No one expected that his diagnosis of lung cancer from his years of painting would have taken him so quickly.

Sarah's Social Security benefits allowed her to pay her bills and maintain her home. She had a reliable handyman who helped her with everything from blowing out the sprinkler line to minor repairs. She enjoyed her home and didn't want to sell it as long as she could stay in it. Sarah enjoyed playing Bunco with her friends, and during one of their game nights, she learned about reverse mortgages. Her friend Linda had recently gone through the process with her husband and was raving about the reverse mortgage planner who helped her.

Sarah was surprised that her friend Linda had taken out a reverse mortgage and felt comfortable talking about it. Out of curiosity, she asked Linda for the contact information for the reverse mortgage planner, and she reached out to her. She learned that with the new regulations for reverse mortgages, it was much safer than it had been in the past.

She learned that reverse mortgage proceeds were tax-free, which was quite different than the capital gains tax she'd be paying from selling off her coins or the art collection that James had left for her. She liked the idea of allowing those assets to continue to grow in value and potentially even leaving them to their son, Xavier.

Xavier lived in Japan and had no use for their stateside home, but he thought the collections were sentimental and had mentioned he'd rather have those than the home. The reverse mortgage created enough funds to allow Sarah to stay in her home well past age 100. She didn't know if she would make it that long but felt a lot of comfort knowing that she could. The funds would also allow her to continue to hire any help that she needed.

THE SULLIVANS SUPPORTED THE LIFESTYLE OF THEIR DREAMS

Jonathan Sullivan and his wife, Penny, ages 63 and 62, respectively, live in Denver, Colorado. Jonathan is one of a few Colorado natives, while Penny is from Illinois. They made Denver their home together for the last 39 years after being introduced to each other through their parents, who were friends from work and the golf course.

Jonathan spent the majority of his career as a computer programmer, and Penny is a realtor, who lately has chosen to work less but with no intention of retiring. Their "savings first, savings second" mentality allowed them to put away a significant amount of money for their retirement, and they owned their $625,000 home free and clear.

Together, the Sullivans had two grown children, TJ and Melissa. TJ, who was working to build his own business in cable and electronics installation, also had "children" in the form of a pair of Huskies. Melissa is married to Adler, and they have a daughter and son of their own, Chloe and Chase.

Penny and Jonathan were both aware of Home Equity Conversion Mortgage (HECM) plans and knew they'd be leveraging this in retirement. Jonathan even began to call it his "home pension fund." The Sullivans made the decision to take a reverse mortgage so they could have a lump sum to buy a vacation condo in Florida, where they could stay during the cold Colorado winters.

For $150,000, they were able to secure a perfect place for themselves that would allow the snowbird lifestyle they were looking for. They paid cash for their vacation home so they wouldn't have a mortgage payment on it.

They also chose to have a $300 per month funding option, which they used to establish life insurance policies for their grandchildren. The premiums would be covered by the reverse mortgage funds until the grandkids were 18. With the remaining funds, they utilized the line of credit option so they could access the funds if needed, which meant helping their son with any expenses while he built his business and followed his dream.

The Sullivans leveraged their home equity early in retirement as part of their overall strategy. They had done well saving money and were now looking forward to a comfortable retirement, supported even greater by the use of a reverse mortgage.

LEGACY

THE JANSSENS HELPED THEIR SON WITH AN EMERGENCY

Randy and Sue Janssen owned a furniture store in Colorado Springs, CO, where they raised their son, Collin, now 34. When they retired, they were able to sell the business, but not to  their son as they had wished. Instead, Collin had started his own family and was a successful dentist who had moved to California because he loved surfing. Unfortunately, tragedy struck Collin one day when he had an accident while enjoying his favorite hobby.

As a healthy young man, Collin didn't have disability insurance in place, and the Janssens found themselves blazing through their savings rather quickly due to his medical bills and inability to work. Collin's wife had returned to work, but he still needed nursing care. With his student debt still lingering, life was becoming increasingly stressful. He was facing foreclosure, and the strain on the family was difficult for Randy and Sue to watch. They had saved up well to fund their retirement and were considering a way to gift their son some money to help him and his family during this difficult time.

The Janssens met with their personal banker to talk about the options they had. They were surprised when she brought up reverse mortgages because their house was nearly paid off. They looked at some tax ramifications of other options, and none made sense to them. They wanted to offer a gift without having to suffer a severe negative impact on their retirement fund. They wanted their retirement funds to grow, and they had a specific budget for using those funds.

With the reverse mortgage, not only were they able to offer a gift, but they could eliminate their mortgage payment, which freed up more room in their budget to allow their assets to continue to grow. It seemed like a win-win scenario.

Because the reverse mortgage funds were tax-free, this seemed like the best option to them. They closed on their reverse mortgage rather quickly, and they felt good about helping Collin through his emergency, knowing that it was only a temporary problem.

They knew their son would get back on his feet, but they didn't want him to have to dig out from an insurmountable hole. They understood from early in their marriage how a financial loss of any size could hurt a relationship. The Janssens knew this gift to their son would be the support he needed until he could return to work and rebuild his dental practice and his life.

Thankfully, their son didn't lose his house, and he and his wife were able to get their medical bills down to a reasonable sum. Collin returned to work full-time, and his wife also continued to work so they could get their finances under control. The Janssens were happy that they could help without hurting their own future in the process. In fact, they gave themselves a gift, as well, by freeing themselves from their own monthly mortgage payments.

THE JACKSONS PAID FOR THEIR GRANDCHILDREN'S EDUCATION

 Sam and April Jackson lived in upstate New York, where Sam was a full-time insurance agent, and April was a homemaker. Sam was successful in his business and was able to store away what they needed for their retirements in a way that allowed them to take a retirement trip to Italy. In fact, Sam surprised April with the trip, which was something that they had always wanted to do.

While on the trip, the Jacksons discussed their children and grandchildren. They were proud to have put their two children through college, and attributed part of their success to them not having the burden of student loans. Because of it, Sam Jr. was a manager in a marketing firm, his wife, Lisa, was a cosmetologist, and their daughter, Keeley, was a senior in high school. The Jacksons' daughter, Elizabeth, was three years younger than Sam Jr. and was also married and had two children—twins Samuel and Shane, who were entering high school.

The Jacksons felt great about being able to put their kids through college and wanted to extend that gift to their grandchildren, as well. When they first approached their children about utilizing the Home Equity Conversion Mortgage (HECM), their kids were skeptical. They were worried that their parents would lose the house out from under them to the lender. Sam and April were able to explain to them that with the new regulations that wasn't possible.

Sam Jr. and Elizabeth weren't thrilled with the idea and asked to talk with the reverse mortgage planner. With their questions answered, and with the knowledge that the funds would be used for the children's education, they were on board. The biggest thing they learned was that they could benefit right now from the reverse mortgage. With the funds from the reverse mortgage, they could support the grandkids' college investment by tapping the equity within their family home tax-free.

The Jacksons felt that the best legacy they could leave wasn't a house, but rather an education, and their children agreed. Sam Jr. and Elizabeth hope to do the same for their grandkids one day. Now, Sam and April are deciding on their next trip, with Australia in their sights.

THE BERNALS CREATED A MEMORY

 The Bernals looked forward to retirement and wanted to celebrate with the whole family. They chuckled whenever they thought of the elaborate plan they had made. This was the year that Lee, a lifelong pharmacist, was retiring. His coworkers were planning him a celebration with cake, but Lee and Lorraine had a big family surprise they were also cooking up. At Christmas, they would announce to their 4 children and 13 grandchildren that they were all—yes, ALL—going to Disney World® in Florida. Lee and Lorraine couldn't wait for the look of surprise on their faces.

They had worked with a travel agent to put all the pieces together. The plan was to rent a house that could accommodate all of them, and they were going to live it up! The Bernals had learned several years ago about the benefit of putting their home equity to use and were giddy with excitement. A family trip would build the memories they wanted to share with their family, and then, in a few more years, they'd consider whether they wanted to sell their house and downsize, or stay put.

They wanted at least five to ten more years in the home, but then they were open to heading anywhere in the world that was calling them. Until then, they wanted to celebrate the beginning of the rest of their lives with a big bang.

Lorraine had been a homemaker when she and Lee were married, a sacrifice that meant they didn't have money for elaborate family vacations. Lorraine had given countless hours to PTA and driving the kids to and from activities for 27 years. Since the youngest had left home, she spent time keeping the house beautiful, as she always had done, and giving her time to school drama programs by sewing costumes.

When grandkids came along, she jumped right back into involvement with them and their activities. The kids loved Nana's house because she also would sew them costumes, just like she had done for her own kids— everything from pirate outfits to princess dresses. The trip to Disney® wasn't something that only the children wanted to do; it was something she always longed to do as well, and didn't mind admitting how excited she was to see the princesses and their beautiful dresses.

The entire Bernal family was indeed surprised at the announcement at Christmas, and are looking forward to their trip in the summer.

JODY CAREY CARED FOR HER MOTHER

 Jody loved being an EMT. She found it challenging but also rewarding and couldn't imagine herself doing anything different. Her father had passed away six years ago, and her mother, Gretchen, now 82, was struggling to stay in their home alone. At 62, Jody was close to retirement but didn't know how she could support her mom on her retirement funds on a single income. Her mom was also on limited income, and she wondered the best route to take.

For the last ten years, Jody owned a condo that was just enough space for her and her two cats, Dash and Ditto, but there wasn't much room for her mom to come live with her. Gretchen, however, had a nice three-bedroom house. Jody took her concerns to her financial advisor: Should she sell both her condo and her mom's home to find something new?

Jody and the financial advisor reviewed several options and scenarios. Because Gretchen's house was mortgage free and Jody still had 20 years of payments, it would save her money to sell the condo and move into Gretchen's home. However, in order for the home to be useful, they would need to make modifications so that Jody could better care for Gretchen. Gretchen had expressed her desire to stay in her home as long as possible rather than move into a nursing home. Jody wanted to honor that for her mom, and for her dad, who asked Jody not to sell the house until after Gretchen couldn't live there anymore.

Jody agreed to sell the condo, but when she moved into the house, she realized how much updating and care it needed. Since Dad had passed, her mom hadn't kept the house up as well as needed. She spent money on renovations and upkeep and worried how that would impact her own financial situation in retirement. Without children to care for her, Jody wondered how she could make ends meet. Again, she went to her financial advisor, and this time he suggested she look into a reverse mortgage on her mom's home.

Jody didn't like the idea of losing her mom's house after she passed, but the reverse mortgage planner explained that Jody still had the right to purchase or sell the home at that time, paying off the reverse mortgage just as she paid off her traditional mortgage when she sold her condo. Instead of having a large mortgage that's reduced through small payments, a reverse mortgage provides tax-free cash flow payments to the homeowner. This means that when Gretchen is no longer able to live there, due to illness or death, Jody could sell the home to pay the debt and keep any remaining equity.

Jody explained this to her mother, who felt it was a great solution that helped both her and her daughter, and the two met with the reverse mortgage planner for further counseling on the matter.

Today, Jody is able to care for her mother in a home that works for them both, while having additional cash flow to cover their expenses. When her mom passes, she intends to sell the home and move back into a condo that better fits her and her lifestyle. In the meantime, Jody is thankful she can help her mom by utilizing a reverse mortgage.

HAROLD DAVIDSON HELPED HIS DAD

Harold's mother had passed away nearly eight years ago, and his father, Dennis, was 87 years old and requiring more income as the cost of living continued to climb. When his mom passed, Harold had purchased a condo for his dad with the insurance money, but he saw that his dad no longer did the things he loved due to his lack of funds. A single dad, Harold considered selling the condo and moving his father in with him and his daughter to help reduce her expenses. Dennis said he'd made friends at the condo and enjoyed living independently, but he was willing to move if it was the only choice.

Harold decided to look at loan options, such as a home equity line of credit and a reverse mortgage. After considering the alternatives, he brought them to his father. The home equity line of credit (HELOC) would require monthly payments, something his already-tight budget couldn't manage, and despite his love for his son and granddaughter, he liked the idea of having his own space. He also loved that he could simply walk to activities and visit with friends. Dennis wanted to stay in his own home.

Dennis was most interested in the reverse mortgage option but had a ton of questions. He was determined to find the "loopholes," but his biggest concern was the fear that he would lose his home if the value dropped.

The reverse mortgage planner explained how the new HECM program worked. One of the benefits is that, despite what happens in the real estate market, Dennis' equity is protected. He also explained how he would never be liable for more than the home was worth and would be able to stay in his home as long as he wanted. It seemed like the perfect solution for his situation, as it would also provide monthly cash flow to help cover expenses. Although Harold was willing to move his father into his home, he appreciated that his dad wanted his independence.

Harold also realized that spending more time with his dad could be good for them all. He makes it a regular practice for his daughter, dad, and him to do activities together and has noticed that he doesn't seem as burdened as before. He's glad his daughter can build a stronger relationship with her grandfather, and he looks forward to being together for many more years to come.

GINA SINGLETON USED A POWER OF ATTORNEY

 Gina had moved into her folks' home to care for her aging parents, but her dad had recently passed away. Now that he was gone, she and her mom were struggling to make the mortgage payment. Fortunately, Mom had equity in her home, and Gina had read about reverse mortgages, so she decided to look into them.

Gina went on Facebook and asked if anyone could recommend a reverse mortgage planner. A friend who worked as a title representative saw some of the answers Gina had received and told her to work with a local, licensed professional. At the title representative's suggestion, she made an appointment with a local professional who specializes in reverse mortgages.

When she sat down with the reverse mortgage planner, she knew how reverse mortgages worked and was able to ask intelligent questions. She shared that the only way she and her mom could stay in the home was to do a reverse mortgage.

As the reverse mortgage planner and Gina chatted, Gina shared that she'd been caring for her parents for several months around the clock and was physically and emotionally exhausted. She was hoping some money from the reverse mortgage could be used to hire in-home help for her mom to give Gina some much-needed relief.

The numbers simply made sense. With a reverse mortgage, the $1423 a month mortgage payment would be eliminated, giving Mom enough money to pay for the property taxes and homeowners insurance as well home maintenance. There was also enough equity to pay for a part-time, in-home care professional to help Gina care for her mom, who suffered from dementia.

Gina had secured a power of attorney earlier in the year when she observed her mother slipping mentally. Gina did her best to explain to her mom about reverse mortgages and felt as if her mom had a grasp of how it could help her remain in her home and relieve some of the financial pressure.

Once the loan closed, Gina and her mom had a party to celebrate the joy and relief they felt of no longer having a monthly mortgage payment. They expressed that they had hoped they could continue to live in Mom's home and provide the care that she needs in her advanced years.

Gina has become an evangelist for reverse mortgages, telling all of the neighbors and her mom's friends about the positive impact a reverse mortgage has had on their lives. Gina's goal for her mom is to remain in her home for as long as possible and live out her days comfortably.

FINAL WORDS: WHERE DO YOU GO FROM HERE?

Although some of the stories in this book are fictional, they are based on real-life, situational reasons that hundreds of thousands of homeowners have used a reverse mortgage to improve their lives. As a reverse mortgage planner, I'm here to support you in your search for answers to determine if a reverse mortgage will meet your goals and dreams.

I'll help you understand the application process, qualification needs, and fees, along with how you can access your equity and more with a confidential, complimentary analysis. **If a reverse mortgage isn't right for you, you are under no obligation to move forward.** Our team has helped several hundred families obtain and utilize the equity in their home. I appreciate the opportunity to help you, your friends, and your family to do the same.

To learn more about reverse mortgages, visit:

http://www.ReverseMortgageRevolution.com
(Reverse Mortgage Resources)

http://bit.ly/1a44pKT
(FHA Reverse Mortgage Information Page)

NRMLA Code of Ethics & Professional Responsibility

This NRMLA Code of Ethics and Professional Responsibility (Code of Ethics) describes values shared and rules applicable to all members of the National Reverse Mortgage Lenders Association (NRMLA). Under this Code of Ethics, NRMLA members generally are responsible and will be held responsible for the actions or failures to act of their officers, directors, employees, agents, and representatives.

As a condition of membership, all NRMLA members are required to adhere to this Code of Ethics. Accordingly, each NRMLA member agrees to observe, maintain, and adhere to the following set of values:

Value 1: Fairness
NRMLA members shall treat consumers with respect and dignity, and in a manner that is fair, reasonable, and as they would want to be treated.

Value 2: Confidentiality
NRMLA members shall appropriately respect, protect, preserve, and safeguard the privacy and confidentiality of information obtained from and about consumers.

Value 3: Integrity
NRMLA members shall act with integrity by adhering to the letter and spirit of this Code of Ethics, which includes disclosing potential conflicts of interest to consumers in a timely basis.

Value 4: Competence
NMRLA members shall provide services to consumers in a competent manner, acquiring and maintaining necessary and appropriate knowledge, skills, and experience to do so, and referring consumers to others who possess such knowledge, skills, and experience when they are unable to do so.

Value 5: Diligence
NRMLA members shall provide services to consumers with diligence and due care promptly, thoughtfully, in a manner considerate of the interests of consumers, and fully in compliance with all applicable legal and regulatory requirements.

Value 6: Professionalism
NRMLA members' conduct shall reflect positively on NRMLA, the profession, and the industry.

ENDORSEMENTS

As a financial advisor for almost 25 years, I have come to appreciate the importance of reverse mortgages as a planning tool for my clients. From retirement income planning, Social Security timing, to estate planning, a reverse mortgage can be a valuable tool, if used properly. Kevin Guttman and his team have been instrumental in helping me understand how reverse mortgages work and the multiple planning options available to my clients. I highly recommend anyone considering a reverse mortgage to talk with Kevin and his team.

Michael Morrow – President, Aspen Creek Wealth Strategies

As a realtor, I am always looking for ways to benefit my clients. My goal is to help them get the most home for their money. That's why I believe strongly in reverse mortgages. For a homebuyer age 62 or older, they can double their buying power with a reverse mortgage. The best part is, with a reverse mortgage, the borrower will never have a mortgage payment! I send all my people to Kevin Guttman, a reverse mortgage planner whom I have known since 2001.

Steve Caruthers – Realtor, Top Realty Group

My father had worked in the same factory for over 40 years. The company pension plan was somehow eliminated when the company was purchased by a foreign competitor—he was relying on Social Security to make ends meet. Once he was able to obtain a reverse mortgage, his whole life improved. He was able to afford to travel and see my family twice before he passed away. My kids still recall when Grandpa came to visit! I tell my clients to consider adding cash flow in retirement by using their 'home pension fund.'

Mark Olsen – Insurance Agent, Farmers Insurance

I firmly believe in a Reverse Mortgage as one possible way to fund a Long-Term Care Protection Plan. The financial features of the current Reverse Mortgage product can provide incredible benefits and should not be overlooked because of past perceptions. It has become a great financial tool that deserves a second look and Kevin is the one that can provide the education needed to determine if it is right for you.

Tom Rasmussen – President, Clear Solutions Insurance Services

www.ingramcontent.com/pod-product-compliance
Lightning Source LLC
Chambersburg PA
CBHW060147200526
45165CB00023B/965